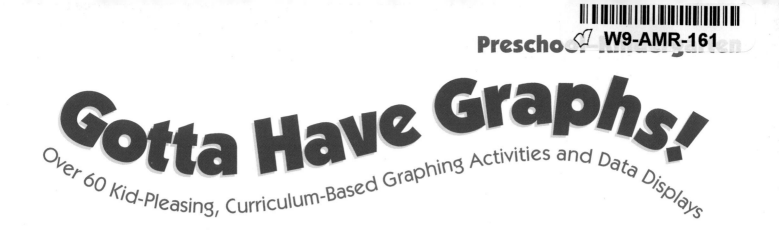

Gotta Have Graphs!
Over 60 Kid-Pleasing, Curriculum-Based Graphing Activities and Data Displays

Table of Contents

www.themailbox.com

©2002 The Education Center, Inc.
All rights reserved.
ISBN #1-56234-510-9

Manufactured in the United States
10 9 8 7 6 5 4 3 2 1

About This Book

Facilitating young children's natural curiosity is part of every teacher's job. Providing graphing activities that engage students in posing and answering questions is a great way to enhance this curiosity. Having students collect, organize, display, and interpret data can also help develop young childrens' critical-thinking skills, which is important in today's information-rich society.

Gotta Have Graphs! makes real-life math fun and easy. Each of the 15 units contains a variety of engaging, hands-on graphing activities designed to supplement and enhance your curriculum. The variety of realistic activities will help your students gain experience with many different types of graphs and data displays, including object graphs, picture graphs, symbol graphs, bar graphs, glyphs, and Venn diagrams. Preparation for each graphing activity is a breeze! Easy-to-follow teacher instructions are provided as well as sample illustrations of completed graphs and data displays. Each graphing activity uses easy-to-obtain data, such as eye color, favorite food, or number of pockets in clothing. The completed graphs provide eye-catching and thought-provoking displays with plenty of opportunities for student interpretation. It's skill-building, it's easy, and it's fun— you've gotta have graphs!

How to Use This Book

Gotta Have Graphs! includes over 60 cross-curricular graphing activities that are perfect for introducing lessons, enhancing lessons, or culminating lessons. *Gotta Have Graphs!* is flexible, allowing you to choose graphing activities to correlate with your teaching themes or to meet your specific curriculum needs. To help you quickly find just the right graphing activity, we've labeled the top of each activity with the type of graph featured.

While using this book, keep these helpful tips in mind:

- **Encourage** active student participation and discussion while collecting and sorting data. Invite youngsters to predict the outcome. These simple steps will help students begin to see themselves as logical, mathematical thinkers.

- **Promote** active student participation in the construction of each graph. Have students think of titles for each graph. When constructing bar graphs, help students determine appropriate labels for the vertical and horizontal axes of the graphs.

- **Discuss** a graph's results with your students. Guide youngsters in comparing the results, looking for relationships and patterns, and then drawing conclusions. Ask open-ended questions and encourage children to answer them fully. These concluding steps will help students develop important critical-thinking skills.

- **Display** the completed graphs for several days (as space permits). Provide time for students to study the display and talk about the graphs with classmates.

Types of Graphs Featured in This Book

Object Graph
Object graphs (sometimes called real graphs) are created using actual objects. This type of concrete graph helps young students compare and build on their understanding of more and less. In an object graph, the objects must be the same size and shape, or they should be placed on a uniform grid to avoid misleading the reader.

Picture Graph
Picture graphs (sometimes called pictographs) are constructed using magazine pictures, photographs, or illustrations to represent real things. In a picture graph, the pictures must be the same size and shape, or they should be placed on a uniform grid to avoid misleading the reader.

Symbolic Graph
Symbolic graphs are the most abstract type of graph because they are are constructed using symbols, such as tally marks or pattern blocks, that represent the items being graphed. In a symbolic graph, the symbols must be the same size and shape, or they should be placed on a uniform grid to avoid misleading the reader.

Bar Graph
Bar graphs use vertical or horizontal parallel bars to compare information from several categories. Each bar stands for a different category. The length of each bar represents a numerical count for that category. A bar graph contains a title as well as labels for the vertical and horizontal axes.

Other Data Displays Featured in This Book

Glyph
Glyphs are pictorial displays of information. Each detail of the picture represents a different piece of information. A glyph guide should accompany a glyph so that it can be interpreted by others.

Venn Diagram
A Venn diagram is a set of interlocking circles that shows relationships between sets of objects. Each circle is labeled for the data inside it. If data belongs in more than one circle, it's placed in the section where the circles overlap. Data that doesn't belong in either circle is placed outside the circles.

Apples Aplenty!

Take a big juicy bite of graphing with these awesome apple activities.

Object Graph

Apple Hues

Graphing apples by color is a fun way to make an object graph with your students. There are many different types of apples, and each one represents a shade or mixture of red, yellow, and green. To prepare, gather a class supply of apples, making sure that you vary the number of each type. During a group time, spread a blank grid on the floor. (Use a permanent marker to draw one on a shower curtain or vinyl tablecloth.) Invite each child to choose an apple and place it on the graph according to color, creating new columns when necessary. As a class, decide on a label for each column. Also ask the class to think of a good title for the graph. Then label the graph accordingly. Conclude by discussing the graph's results. It's as easy as apple pie!

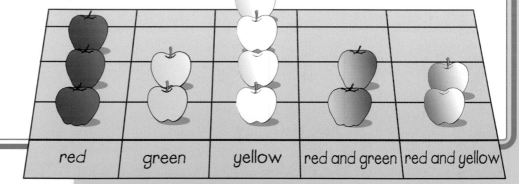

| red | green | yellow | red and green | red and yellow |

Symbolic Graph

How Sweet It Is...

Or is it? Set up the following taste test and invite your youngsters to decide whether they like their apples sweet or tart. Ahead of time, prepare a two-column graph on tagboard as shown. Provide a spring-type clothespin for each child and a red and a green marker to share. Cut two red Delicious apples and two green Granny Smith apples into bite-size pieces. (Adjust the number of apples according to class size.) To begin the activity, ask your students whether they like sweet or tart apples. Then have the class predict whether more students will like tart or sweet. Next, have each child taste both types of apples. Then ask her to draw a red or green dot on her clothespin to correspond with her apple preference. Next, have each child clip her clothespin onto the chart in the appropriate column. When all of the students have indicated their choices on the graph, discuss the results. What's the favorite—sweet or tart?

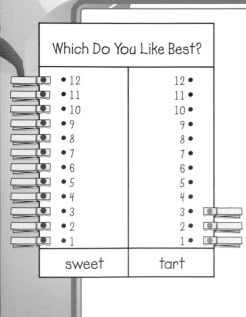

Which Do You Like Best?

| sweet | tart |

Picture Graph
Centered on Seeds

Further your apple explorations by finding out how many seeds are in different types of apples. In advance, program a graph similar to the one shown. Duplicate and cut out a construction paper seed (page 6) for each child. To begin, give each child an apple. Then ask, "How many seeds are in an apple?" Allow students to share their estimates. Then have an adult helper assist each child in removing the seeds from his apple. Instruct the child to count the total number of seeds in his apple and then glue them to his seed pattern. Have him write his name on the seed pattern. Next, have him glue his cutout in the correct column on the graph. When the recording is finished, encourage children to interpret the graph's results. "Seed-sational!"

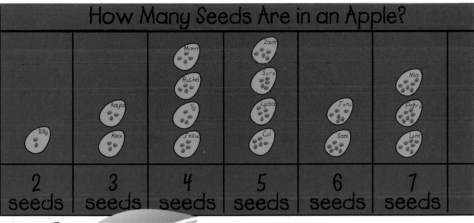

How Many Seeds Are in an Apple?

Bar Graph
Apples Here, Apples There

Apple foods are everywhere! Help your youngsters experience a variety of apple options with this activity. To prepare, copy the pictures on page 7. Color and cut out the pictures; then use each one to label a different row on a graph as shown.

To begin the activity, have students share some of their favorite ways to eat apples. Then share with the class the prepared graph. Read aloud the six apple options. Then encourage each student to choose her favorite one and then indicate her choice by coloring a space on the graph. To extend this activity, ask another class to do the same activity; then compare the resulting graphs. Are they the same? How are the graphs different?

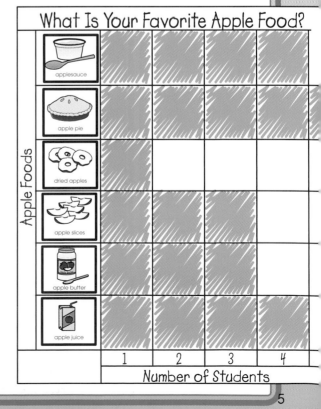

What Is Your Favorite Apple Food?

Seed Patterns

Use with "Centered on Seeds" on page 5.

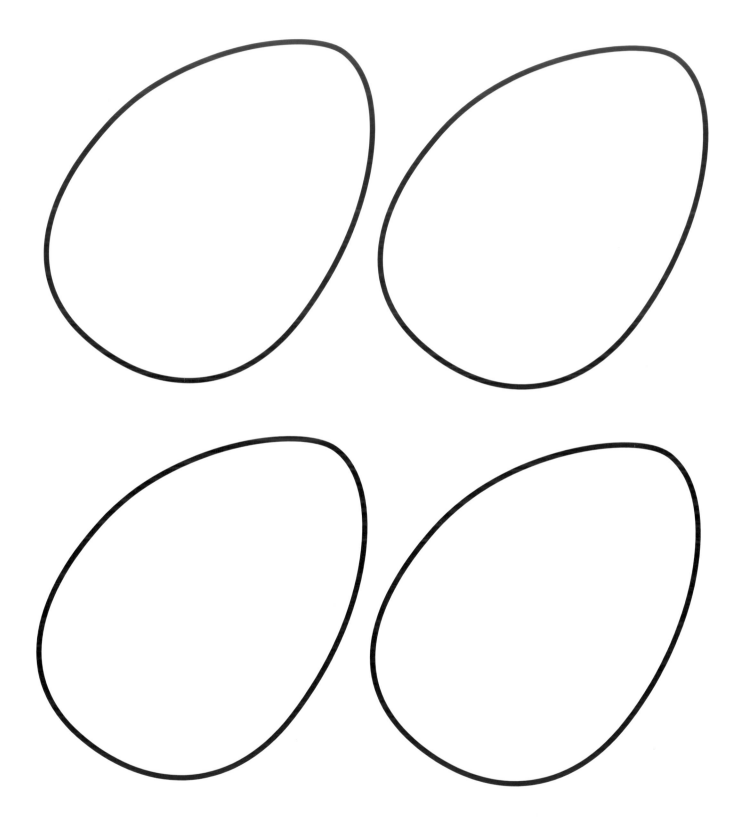

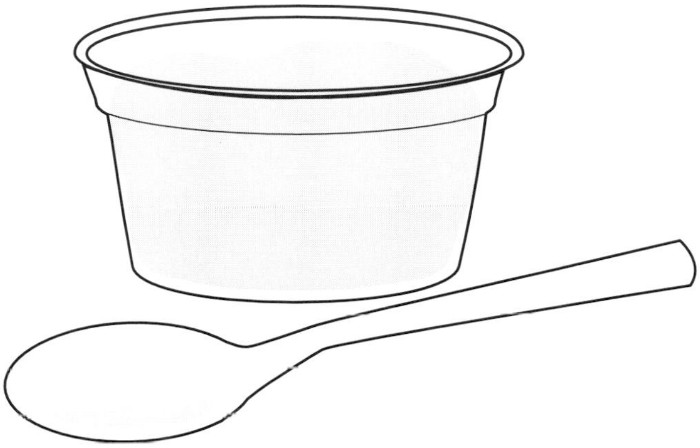

applesauce

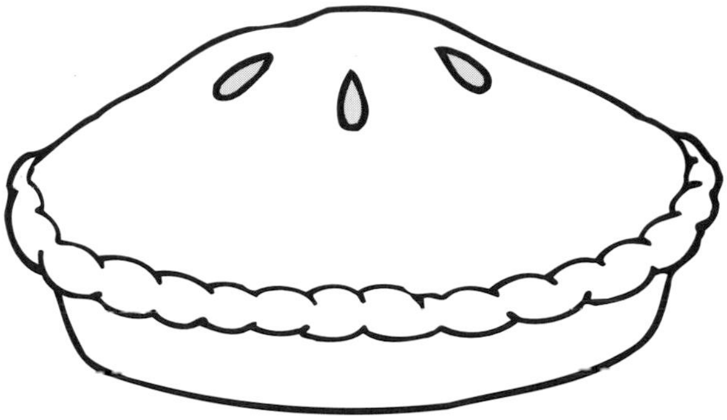

apple pie

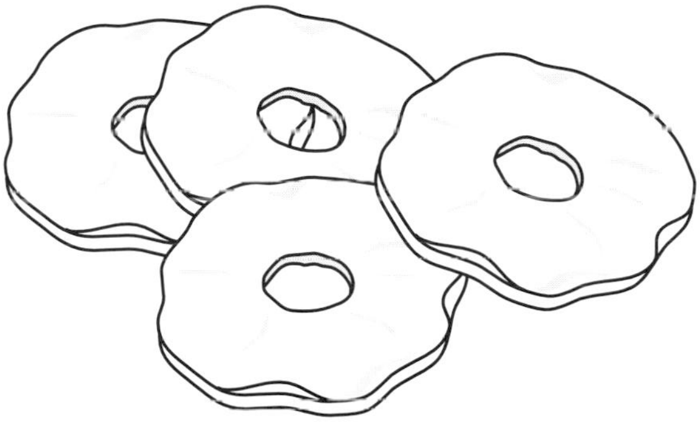

dried apples

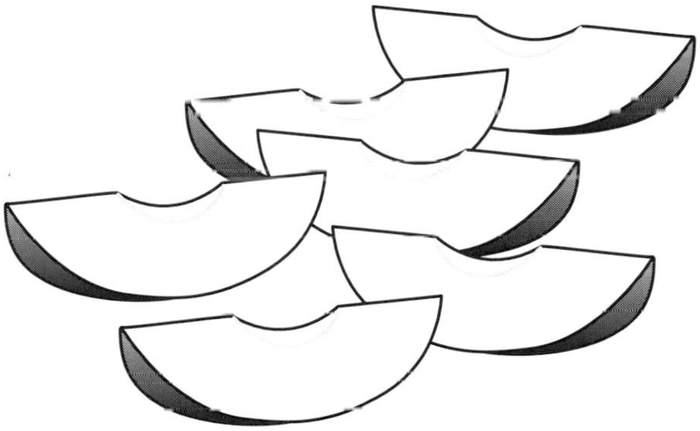

apple slices

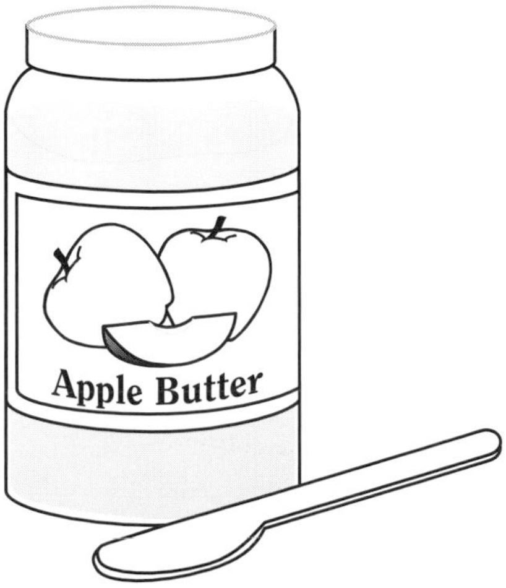

apple butter

Apple Butter

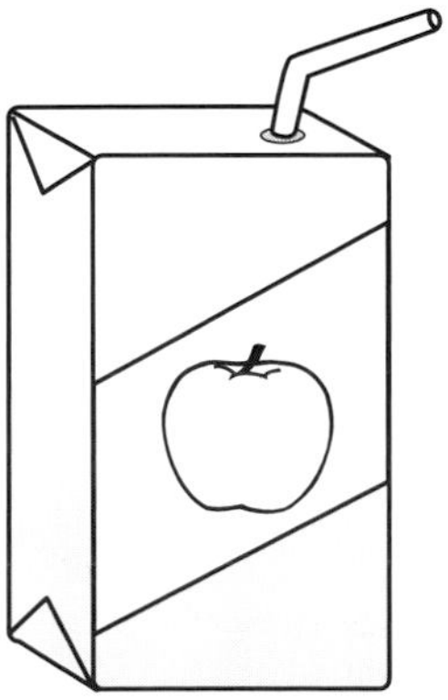

apple juice

Colors All Around

Colors here. Colors there. Color graphing everywhere!

Picture Graph

Crayon Colors

What's the most popular color among your students' favorites? Let's find out! In advance, program a graph with one column for each color as shown. Also, duplicate the crayon patterns on page 10 to make a class supply; then cut them apart. To begin the activity, give one crayon pattern to each child. Instruct the child to color her pattern to match her favorite color. Then ask her to tape her pattern to the appropriate column on the graph. So what *is* the most popular color? How about the second most popular? Is there one color that was nobody's favorite?

What's Your Favorite Crayon Color?

| red | orange | green | blue | yellow | purple |

Venn Diagram

Sorting Colors

Venn diagrams make great tools for slightly more sophisticated sorting activities! To prepare, choose two different colors and then gather a collection of fabric swatches, wallpaper squares, and/or paint chips, many of which contain one or both of the colors you chose. On a sheet of bulletin board paper, draw two large intersecting circles—one in each color that you chose for your color collection. Label the diagram similar to the one shown; then mount it on a bulletin board.

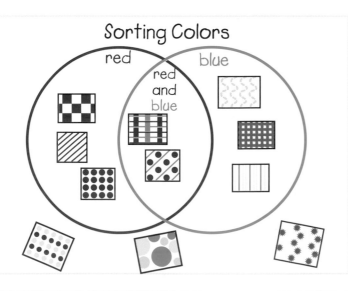

Sorting Colors

red   blue

red
and
blue

Hold up one color piece at a time and have a student volunteer determine whether that piece has one, both, or neither of the colors in it. Help her pin the swatch to the corresponding area of the Venn diagram. When the color collection is completely sorted, count and compare the number in each area. Afterward, remove all the color samples and encourage children to repeat the activity independently during center time.

Bar Graph

The Long and Short of It

This graphing activity has your youngsters examining color words. Draw and label a graph on chart paper similar to the one shown. Ask your students to think of color words. When a child names a color word, help him write it in one of the blocks on the left-hand side of the graph. Then ask the child to count the number of letters in the word. Next, have him color that number of boxes to the right of the color word with the corresponding color. Continue with as many color words as your students can think of. Then discuss the results of the graph with your students. Which color word has the fewest letters? How many have six letters? Does one color word have the most letters?

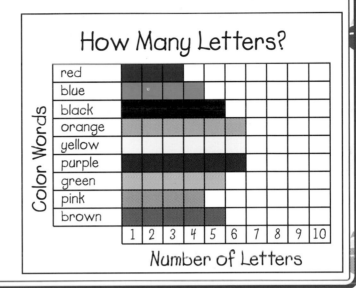

How Many Letters?

Symbolic Graph

Roll It!

This center activity combines probability and graphing in one colorful lesson! To prepare, cover a cube-shaped tissue box with white construction paper; then use markers to make a different-colored circle on each side of the cube: red, yellow, blue, orange, green, and purple. Put this color die in a center, along with copies of the reproducible on page 11.

To do this activity, ask a child to write his name on two reproduced pages. Instruct him to number the graphs "1" and "2." Have him roll the die and then color a dot of that color in the corresponding column on Graph 1. Have him repeat this procedure for a total of ten rolls. Then ask him to predict what the results will be if he does the same activity with Graph 2. Invite him to complete Graph 2 in the same manner with another set of ten rolls. Encourage him to examine the two graphs. What color came up most often on the first graph? The second one? How are the two graphs similar and how are they different?

9

Crayon Patterns
Use with "Crayon Colors" on page 8.

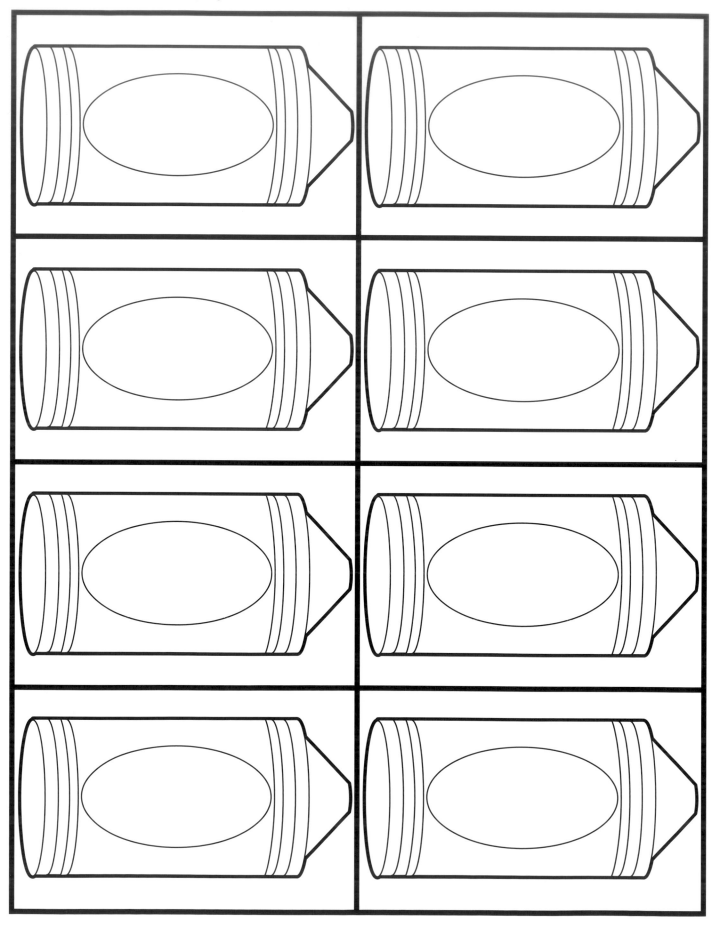

Graph Number _____

red	yellow	blue	orange	green	purple

All About Us

What could be a more interesting topic for your youngsters than themselves? Use these graphing ideas to help youngsters learn about their class and individual classmates.

Picture Graph

Boys and Girls

Are there more boys or more girls in your class? Invite youngsters to find out with this simple graphing activity. Duplicate the child patterns on page 15 to make a class supply. Then instruct each child to color the pattern to resemble herself (or himself) and cut it out. Label a length of bulletin board paper as shown. As each student finishes her cutout, have her tape it to the graph in the appropriate column. When all the cutouts are on the graph, discuss the results. Are there more boys or girls in the class? How many more? If you (the teacher) add your own cutout to the graph, how do the results change?

More Girls or More Boys?

GIRLS						

BOYS						

Object Graph

The Eyes Have It

Here's a different kind of graph that uses real people to show students what portion of your class has which eye color! To prepare, use masking tape to create a graph on the floor similar to the one shown. Then label four sheets of drawing paper, each with a different eye color. Place each sheet at the bottom of the graph as shown. Next, instruct each student to stand on a separate block on the graph in the column that represents his or her eye color. When every student is positioned, the graph will be complete! Discuss what the graph reveals. For added interest, ask another class to make its own eye color graph. How do the two graphs compare?

brown

blue

green

other

Birthday Bows

Which month has the most birthdays? To find out, have your students complete the following object graph. To prepare, label a length of bulletin board paper as shown. Then mount the paper to a wall space or on a bulletin board. To complete the graph, give each youngster a self-sticking bow. Have each child stick her bow in the appropriate row that shows her birth month. Then have the student write her name below her bow. Once all the bows are attached, discuss with your students what the graph reveals. This object graph doubles as a colorful display to show off youngsters' birthday months!

Which Month Has the Most Birthdays?

January	February	March	April	May
Ben				Eddie
Sue			Sara	Jenny
Terry	Rayna		Bob	Helen
Liz	Duncan	Mike	Debbie	Mark

Name Numbers

Who has a long name? Who has a short one? Children can compare and contrast the number of letters in their names with this picture graph. First, duplicate the letter-counting reproducible on page 15 for each child. Have each child print her name on the reproducible, writing one letter in each box. (If anyone needs more than ten letter spaces, just glue on an extension!) On a length of bulletin board paper, draw a simple graph and label the columns as shown. Have each child tape her name to the graph in the appropriate column. Talk about what the graph reveals. Whose name is longest? Shortest? What's the most common number of letters in a name?

How Many Letters Are in Your Name?

1 Letter	2 Letters	3 Letters	4 Letters	5 Letters	6 Letters	7 Letters	8 Letters	9 Letters	10 Letters
				Grant					
			Jean	Lissa				Jonathan	
			Mark	Carey	Steven				
		Dot	Luke	Jahna	Susann	Morgana	Rosalina	Naquitana	
AJ	Max	John	John	Elisa	Stuart	Maryann	Shakisha	Deshaunda	JeanClaude

Bar Graph

How Tall Are You?

Take a simple bar graph to new heights with this idea! First, cut a five-foot length of bulletin board paper. Then create a graph similar to the one shown by drawing a 4$\frac{1}{2}$-foot column for each student. (You may need more than one length of paper if you have a large class.) Label the top of each column with a different child's initials. Draw a bold horizontal line across the columns at the one-foot, two-foot, three-foot, and four-foot marks as shown. Then draw more lines above the three-foot mark to indicate one-inch-high intervals. Attach the graph to a classroom wall, aligning the bottom edge of the paper with the floor.

To complete the graph, measure one student at a time and mark the column under his initials. Ask him to use a crayon to color his column up to his actual height. When every student has recorded his height, discuss what the graph reveals. What a fun way to mix measurement skills and graphing!

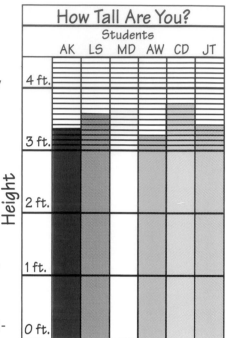

How Tall Are You?

Picture Graph

Lefty or Righty?

Here's a "hand-y" way to display information! Cut a long length of bulletin board paper and label it as shown. Ask each child which hand she writes with more often. Give each student a 4$\frac{1}{2}$" x 6" piece of construction paper. Then paint the palm and fingers of each student's writing hand with washable tempera paint. Next, have each child make a handprint on her construction paper. Then write the student's name below her handprint. Direct the student to glue her handprint on the graph in the corresponding row. When every child has contributed, display the graph and discuss the results. Do you have more lefties or righties in your class?

Are You a Lefty or a Righty?

Letter-Counting Reproducible
Use with "Name Numbers" on page 13.

1	2	3	4	5	6	7	8	9	10

Family Fun

Oh, the graphing possibilities in family fun!

Sibling Situations

How many students have only brothers, only sisters, both, or no siblings at all? Have your students complete the following data display to compare their sibling situations. On a length of bulletin board paper, use two different colors of marker to draw two large intersecting circles; then label the diagram as shown. Next, make photocopies of your students' individual photos and cut them out. Display the Venn diagram and gather students around it. Ask one child at a time to tell whether she has brothers, sisters, both, or neither. Help her tape her photo to the area of the diagram that fits her sibling situation. When everyone has contributed to the diagram, count and compare the photos in each area.

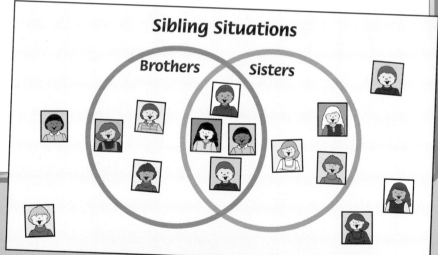

Sibling Situations

Brothers   Sisters

Symbolic Graph

What's Your Place in the Family?

After discussing siblings (see "Sibling Situations"), make this simple graph to find out about the birth order of your students. On your chalkboard, draw a simple graph with four rows and label it as shown. Have each child add a tally mark to the row that reflects his place in his family. When each student has contributed to the graph, discuss the results. Then give each child a chance to talk about why he likes or doesn't like his family position.

What's Your Place in Your Family?	
👧👧👦	ⵘ
👧👦👧	II
👧👦👦	IIII
👦	III

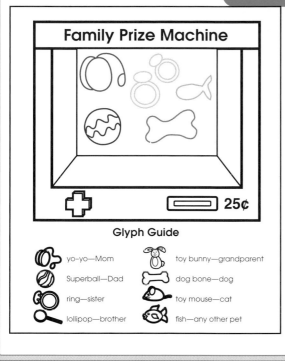

Prize Families

This prize-machine glyph will help students learn about one another's families. Give each child a copy of the prize machine on page 19. Then have students look at the glyph guide at the bottom of the reproducible. Direct the student to draw one item in the prize machine for each corresponding family member or pet. Display the completed glyphs with a large copy of the glyph guide and invite students to compare their families. As an extension, help students use the information on the glyphs to graph the types of family pets or number of family members.

Symbolic Graph

Grandparents Graph

Find out how many of your students have grandparents living with them with this quick graph. On a sheet of chart paper, sketch and label a simple two-column graph as shown. Have each youngster write her name on a sticky note. If she has one or more grandparents living at home, have her place her sticky note in the left-hand column. If she doesn't have grandparents living in her home, have her place her sticky note in the right-hand column. Examine the graph and count the two groups. Have students tell about their grandparents. Whose grandparents live in the same town or city? Whose live far away?

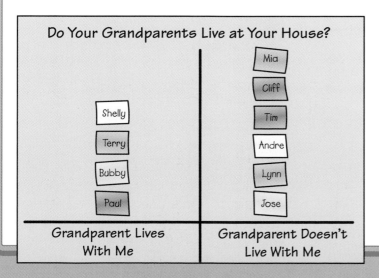

17

Symbolic Graph

Population Exploration

Are there more boys or more girls in all the families represented in your classroom? Make these quick paper-plate graphs and find out! On a white paper plate, draw a simple figure of a man on one half and a simple figure of a woman on the other. Draw a dividing line in the center and then label the plate as shown. (If you have a large class, you might want to work with small groups and make one graph for each group.) Give each child a spring-type clothespin. Help him write his name on one side of the clothespin. Ask him if he has more males or females in his family. Then have him clip his clothespin to the corresponding section of the paper plate. When the graph is complete, encourage the group to discuss the results. If you had several groups each make a different graph, encourage the whole class to compare and contrast all the graphs.

Picture Graph

Pets, Pets, Pets

Do your students have bunches of bunnies? A crew of cats? Or perhaps a lone lizard? Use this graph to find out just how many pets your students' families have. First, ask each child to draw a picture of all of her pets. Have her write the corresponding numeral at the top of her drawing. Ask any student who doesn't have a pet to label a blank sheet of paper with her name and the number 0. Encourage her to decorate the 0 to resemble a pretend pet. Draw several columns on a length of bulletin board paper; then label each column with a number. Write the graph title at the top before displaying the graph on a wall or bulletin board. Have each student tape her picture to the corresponding column to show how many pets are in her family. Discuss the results of the graph. Who has the most pets? The fewest? What number of pets is most popular?

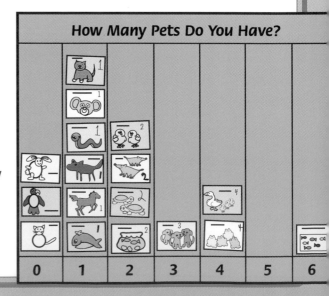

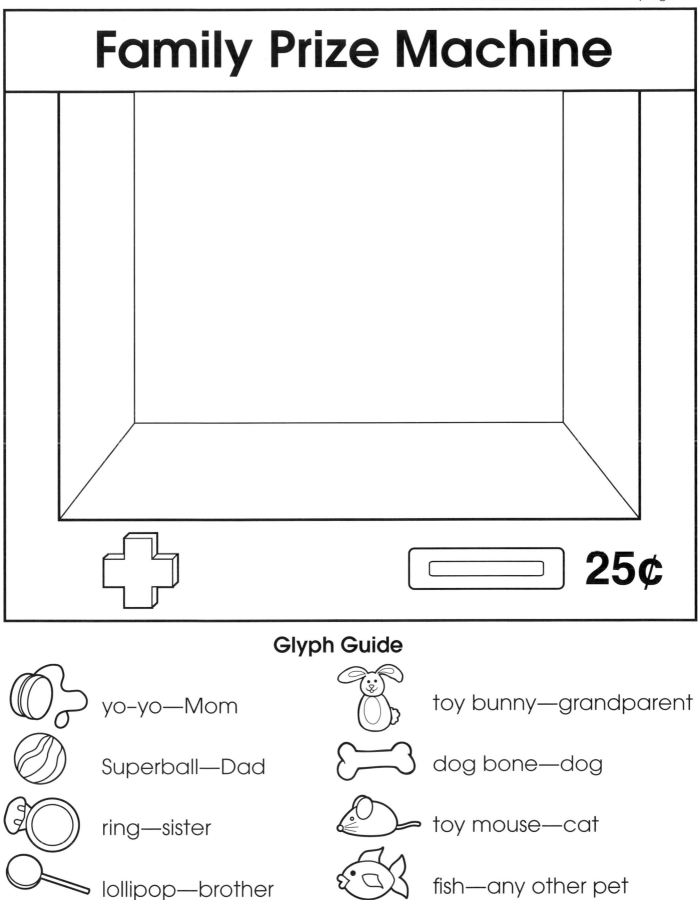

Family Prize Machine

25¢

Glyph Guide

yo-yo—Mom

Superball—Dad

ring—sister

lollipop—brother

toy bunny—grandparent

dog bone—dog

toy mouse—cat

fish—any other pet

Pocket Pizzazz

The learning possibilities are plentiful with pockets!

Symbolic Graph

Count 'em Up!

How many pockets are in your classroom today? That's the question. Students find the answer when they create this graph! To begin, make 11 copies of the pocket pattern on page 22. Label each pocket with a different number from 0 to 10; then cut the pockets out. Glue each pocket to a half sheet of construction paper, leaving the top edge open. Mount the numbered pockets on a wall or bulletin board and label the display with the question "How many pockets are in our classroom today?" To do this activity, have each child count the number of pockets on her clothing. Then have her write her name on a slip of paper and tuck the slip into the pocket with the corresponding number. When every student has contributed to the graph, count the name slips in each pocket and discuss the results.

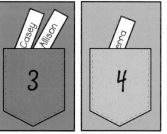

Picture Graph

Pocket Possibilities

Your youngsters will have to dig deep and do a little homework to complete this graph. Give each child a copy of page 23. Instruct him to take the sheet home and ask his family members to empty their pockets. Tell him to look over the pocket contents and choose four items to illustrate, one item in each section of the page. Ask students to return their pages to school the next day.

Have each child cut apart his boxes on the bold lines. In turn, ask each child to show his illustrations and then tape them to a large sheet of bulletin board paper. Create labels on blank index cards as the categories become clear. So what's in most people's pockets?

Object Graph

Pocket Piles

Put youngsters on the lookout for petite pockets with this sorting center. Gather a collection of doll clothes, with and without pockets. Label a tabletop with the two categories shown. Use yarn or tape to make space markers. Encourage a student at this center to look for pockets on each piece of doll clothing and place the article in the corresponding row. What does the graph tell you?

Pockets

No Pockets

Picture Graph

Palatable Pockets

Of course, pockets aren't just for wearing anymore—they're for eating, too! Plan a tasting activity with pocket bread, or pita sandwiches, to help students determine the most popular pocket sandwich in the classroom. To prepare, make a class supply of the pocket bread pattern on page 22. Then make four different kinds of pocket bread sandwiches, such as peanut butter and jelly, chicken salad, turkey, and cheese. Cut each sandwich into little pieces just right for sampling. Label a length of bulletin board paper with the sandwich types; then display it on a wall.

Invite each child to try each kind of sandwich. (Check for food allergies or diet restrictions before serving.) After the tasting, give each child a copy of the pocket bread pattern. Have her draw and color her preferred filling in the opening, and then write her name on the pattern as shown. Invite her to tape her pocket bread picture to the graph in the corresponding column. Which filling flavor do your students favor?

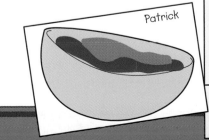

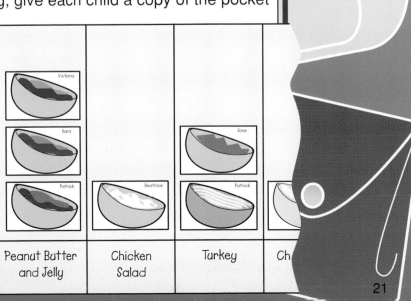

Peanut Butter and Jelly	Chicken Salad	Turkey	Ch

21

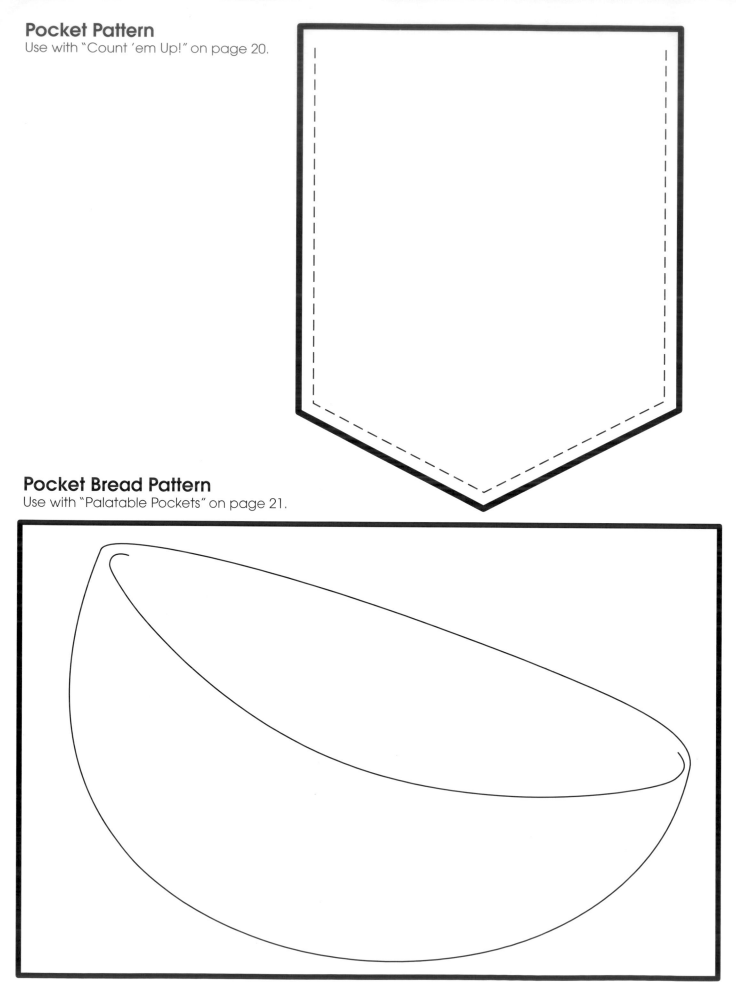

Pocket Pattern
Use with "Count 'em Up!" on page 20.

Pocket Bread Pattern
Use with "Palatable Pockets" on page 21.

What's in People's Pockets?

Note to the teacher: Use with "Pocket Possibilities" on page 20.

23

Plenty of Pumpkins!

This crop of pumpkin-themed activities
is just right for the pickin'!

Bar Graph

Guess and Graph

Introduce your pumpkin-graphing activities with this guessing game. To prepare, make a vertical graph with four four-inch-wide columns. Copy, color, and cut out the mystery item pictures on page 26; then use a different one to label each column. Put a pumpkin inside a sturdy pillowcase and tie a knot in the end of the case. Display the following items on a table: another similarly sized pumpkin, a five-pound bag of flour, an apple, and a small box of cereal.

To begin, explain that you are hiding in the pillowcase something that is shown on the table. Invite each child to grasp the pillowcase by the knot and use both hands to lift it up. Then have him guess which item is hidden in the bag and place a sticky note in the corresponding column on the graph. When each child has guessed, have the class look inside the pillowcase. How many were right? Wrong? What helped you make your guess?

Picture Graph

Sink or Float—Pumpkin Style

Does a pumpkin float like a boat or sink like a stone? To prepare for this prediction activity, make a class supply of the pumpkin patterns on page 26. Also trim the top edge of two long strips of blue bulletin board paper to resemble waves. Write "float" on the left end of one and "sink" on the left end of the other. Ask each child to predict whether a pumpkin will float. If she thinks it will, have her cut out a smiling pumpkin and then tape it to the "float" strip. If not, have her cut out the surprised pumpkin and then tape it to the "sink" strip. After each child has made a prediction, discuss what the graph reveals. Then try it out and see whether a pumpkin floats!

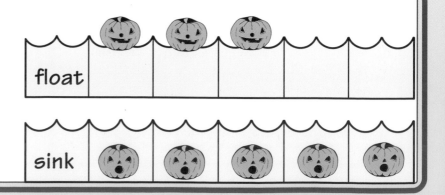

Personal Pumpkins

What are *your* pumpkin time preferences? These glyphs tell the whole story! To prepare, make a class supply of the glyph guide on page 27. Provide crayons, markers, construction paper (lots of orange and black), scissors, and glue. Have each child cut out a large construction paper pumpkin. Then help him complete his glyph by following the glyph guide. When the pumpkins are finished, mount them on a bulletin board background of pumpkin vines. Be sure to post a key with the glyphs so visitors can interpret the glyphs. As an extension, have students graph information revealed in the glyphs, such as "How many students will dress up for Halloween?" or "How many students like spooky stories?"

Venn Diagram

Seed Tasting

How do your youngsters like their pumpkin seeds—roasted, raw, both, or not at all? To prepare for this center activity, purchase a cup each of raw and roasted pumpkin seeds. Use two different-colored markers to draw and program a Venn diagram on a large sheet of poster board as shown. Put the seeds in separate, labeled bowls and have construction paper and glue nearby. Ask each child to visit the center and taste both types of seeds. Then invite her to cut out a construction paper seed, write her initials on it, and glue it on the diagram according to her preference. After each child has glued on a seed, discuss what the diagram reveals. Are pumpkin seeds a class favorite?

How Do You Like Your Seeds?

roasted

raw

both

GR JN TO WE WD
AR LM TR JT FP
MN KO AW OP TF AS
RL

25

Mystery Item Patterns
Use with "Guess and Graph" on page 24.

Pumpkin Patterns
Use with "Sink or Float—Pumpkin Style" on page 24.

Personal Pumpkins
Glyph Guide

Stem	Hair
I am a girl.	I like pumpkin pie.
I am a boy.	I do not like pumpkin pie.

Eyes	Cheeks
I have visited a pumpkin farm.	I have tasted pumpkin seeds.
I have not visited a pumpkin farm.	I have not tasted pumpkin seeds.

Teeth	Nose
I have lost a tooth.	For Halloween, I will dress up.
I have not lost a tooth yet.	For Halloween, I will do something else.

Ears	Legs and Feet
I have a pumpkin at home.	I like spooky stories.
I do not have a pumpkin at home.	I do not like spooky stories.

A Seasonal Sampler

Winter, spring, summer, or fall—which do *you* like the best of all?
Let's graph it and see!

Picture Graph

Which Is Your Favorite Season?

To prepare for this idea, photocopy the season labels on page 30 and make a class supply of each of the season markers (page 30). Use the season labels to identify the columns on a four-column graph. To begin this activity, prompt a discussion about the different signs of the seasons where you live. Then ask each child to think about which season is her favorite and why. Next, invite each child to choose the marker corresponding to her favorite season and color it. Then have her glue her marker in the appropriate column on the graph. When each child has indicated her seasonal preference, discuss what the graph reveals. Is your favorite season happening now?

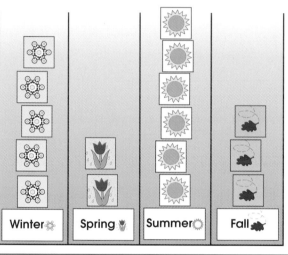

Object Graph

The Season of Your Birth

Most children know the dates of their births, but do they know in which *seasons* they were born? Here's a graph that makes that clear. In advance, make a copy of the season labels on page 30. Tape four strips of colorful construction paper together and use the labels to make a graph. To begin this activity, give each child a new birthday candle. Encourage each child to lay his candle on the graph in the season that corresponds to his birthday. (If you'd like to make the graph more permanent, have each child attach his candle to the graph with a little bit of reusable adhesive.) Now let's look it over. Which season has the most birthdays in it?

Glyph

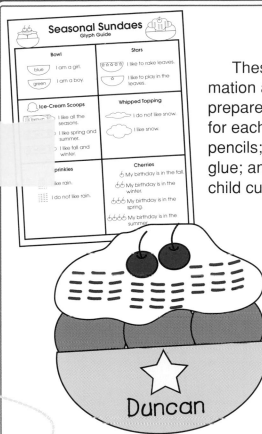

Seasonal Sundaes

These delicious-looking sundaes convey lots of information about your students' seasonal preferences. To prepare, make a copy of the glyph guide on page 31 for each child. Provide crayons, markers, or colored pencils; colorful construction paper scraps; scissors; glue; and a supply of star stickers. Begin by having each child cut out a construction paper ice-cream bowl in the appropriate color (see the glyph guide). Then direct children to follow the rest of the guide to declare their specific seasonal likes and dislikes. When a student has completed his sundae, have him write his name on the bowl. Display the completed glyphs and encourage students to look at them to see what they can find out about their classmates. As an extension, have students graph information gleaned from the glyphs, such as the number of students who don't like snow.

Symbolic Graph

How's the Weather?

What's the weather like in your neck of the woods? This graph will tell it all! For the season you're in now, program a graph with the varying types of weather you are likely to have in your area. (If desired, use the season marker patterns on page 30.)

Each day for a week, ask a child to report on the weather. Have him place sticky notes on the graph corresponding to that day's weather. When the graph is completed use it to discuss how your weather has been. Have students determine the most prevalent weather condition and the least prevalent weather condition.

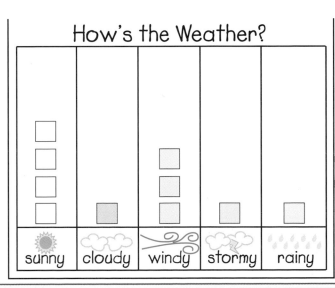

Season Labels and Markers

Use with "Which Is Your Favorite Season?" and "The Season of Your Birth" on page 28.

Seasonal Sundaes

Glyph Guide

Bowl

blue — I am a girl.

green — I am a boy.

Stars

★★★★★ — I like to rake leaves.

☆ — I like to play in the leaves.

Ice-Cream Scoops

brown — I like all the seasons.

pink — I like spring and summer.

white — I like fall and winter.

Whipped Topping

I like rain.

I do not like rain.

Sprinkles

| | | | | | — I do not like snow.

------- — I like snow.

Cherries

🍒 My birthday is in the fall.

🍒🍒 My birthday is in the winter.

🍒🍒🍒 My birthday is in the spring.

🍒🍒🍒🍒 My birthday is in the summer.

Note to the teacher: Use with "Seasonal Sundaes" on page 29.

"Pasta-tively" Graphing

Put pasta on the menu and serve up a heaping
helping of learning fun!

Object Graph

Pasta Colors

Graphing and color sorting combine to make this an interesting pasta activity. In advance, make a class supply of the graph on page 34. Provide a medium bowl of uncooked tricolor pasta and green, orange, and yellow crayons. To do this activity, have a child color the pasta on the graph to match the color words. Then invite him to gently grasp as big a handful of pasta as he can from the bowl. Ask him to sort the pasta onto the graph. Which color has the most? The least?

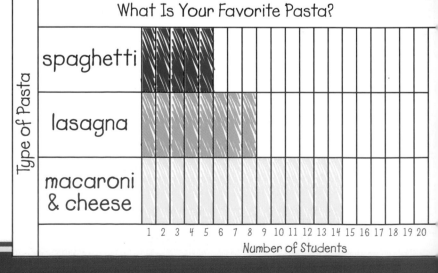

Bar Graph

Your Order, Please?

The bar graph shows the pasta preference! To prepare, create a graph on a large sheet of bulletin board paper similar to the one shown. Gather your students and ask them to think about the three types of pasta dishes shown. (Or even serve a little of each if you're feeling industrious!) Next, have your students group themselves according to their favorite pasta dishes. Give each group a different-colored crayon. Then, one group at a time, have each group member color in a section of the appropriate row on the graph. (Be sure that each group colors spaces that are together on the graph.) When the graph is complete, ask your students, "Without counting, can you tell which pasta dish is the favorite? How about the least favorite?"

Symbolic Graph

Pasta "Pot-pourri"

Visual discrimination makes the mark in this graphing activity. To prepare, photocopy the graph on page 35 to make a class supply. Provide crayons, a ladle, and a large bowl of uncooked penne, elbow, bowtie, and rotini pasta. To do this activity, invite a child to scoop out a ladleful of pasta from the bowl. Then ask him to sort the pasta according to shape, making one tally mark on the graph for each piece of pasta. After each shape has been tallied on the graph, discuss what the graph reveals. Which shape has the most? The second most? Did any shape not have any at all?

Bar Graph

Spaghetti Kids

If you were a spaghetti noodle, how tall would you be? Let's find out! To prepare, gather a supply of uncooked spaghetti noodles and a long sheet of bulletin board paper. Draw a line about three inches from the bottom edge of the paper. Also create a graph similar to the one shown. To do this activity, have students work in pairs. Instruct one child to lie on the paper with his feet on the line. Then have his partner use the spaghetti noodles to measure him. Encourage children to be creative with any remaining space to be measured that turns out to be less than a spaghetti noodle in length. (For example, you might suggest they break the noodle in half or in three same-sized pieces.) Then have the measured child stand up and look at the noodles on the paper. Have him record his height (in noodles) on the graph. (Prompt children to color half of a box for a half noodle, etc.) Wow, how many noodles tall are you?

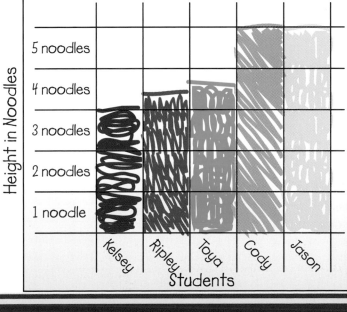

How Many Noodles Tall Are You?

orange	green	yellow

Note to the teacher: Use with "Pasta Colors" on page 32.

Name _____

How many of each pasta shape do you have?

Note to the teacher: Use with "Pasta 'Pot-pourri'" on page 33.

Step Right Up!

Use youngsters' shoes to explore
graphing skills. It's just the right fit!

Picture Graph

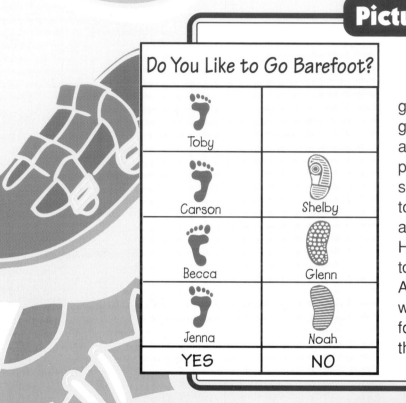

Do You Like to Go Barefoot?	
Toby	
Carson	Shelby
Becca	Glenn
Jenna	Noah
YES	NO

Barefootin'

Find out children's feelings on going barefoot with this activity. Program a length of bulletin board paper as shown. Then use washable paint to paint the bottom of one child's foot or shoe (let parents know ahead of time to dress their children in older shoes) according to the child's preference. Have the child then step onto the grid to make a print in the appropriate space. After the paint dries, have each child write his name below his shoeprint or footprint. Then discuss the results of the graph. What sassy soles!

Bar Graph

Walk It Off

Incorporate more math into your graphs with this measurement activity. Duplicate the recording sheet on page 38 for each child. Gather a supply of yardsticks, jump ropes, and rest towels or mats. Then designate one storage shelf for students to use in the activity. Have each child measure how many steps long each item is. (Encourage him to step heel to toe.) Then instruct the child to record the number of steps on his sheet to make a graph. After everyone has completed a graph, encourage students to compare their graphs and find differences. Then challenge students to figure out why there might be such differences. Ready, set...step!

Symbolic Graph

Got Laces?

Buckles, Velcro, laces...what's on your students' shoes? Find out with this simple graph. Create a chart on a sheet of poster board, similar to the one shown. Staple a different shoelace under each heading. Personalize a spring-type clothespin for each child. To complete the graph, have the child look down at her shoes and then clip her pin to the lace in the appropriate column. Summarize the graph's results on a separate piece of paper. Then do the graph again for the next few days to see if the results change from day to day.

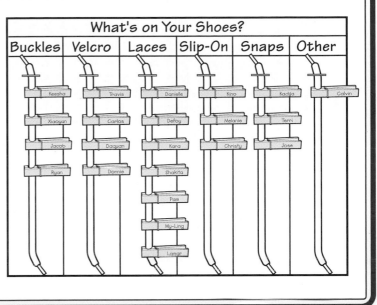

Bar Graph

Shoes, Shoes, Shoes

This parent-involvement activity will have little supersleuths on the lookout for shoes. Copy a parent note (page 39) for each child. Send the notes home to ask parents to help their children count pairs of shoes they find around the house. Once the completed tally sheets are sent in, graph the results. Help students interpret the data by having students explain why some students found more shoes than others. (A student with a large family would find more shoes.) Wow, that's a LOT of shoes!

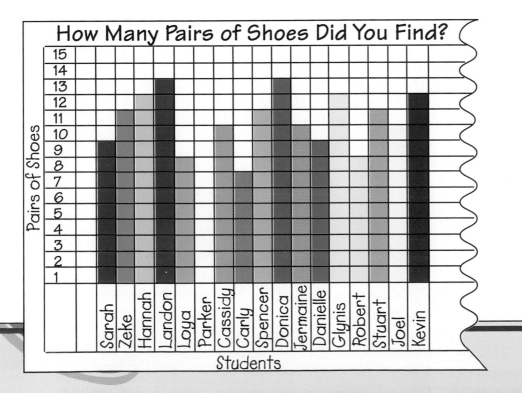

How Long?

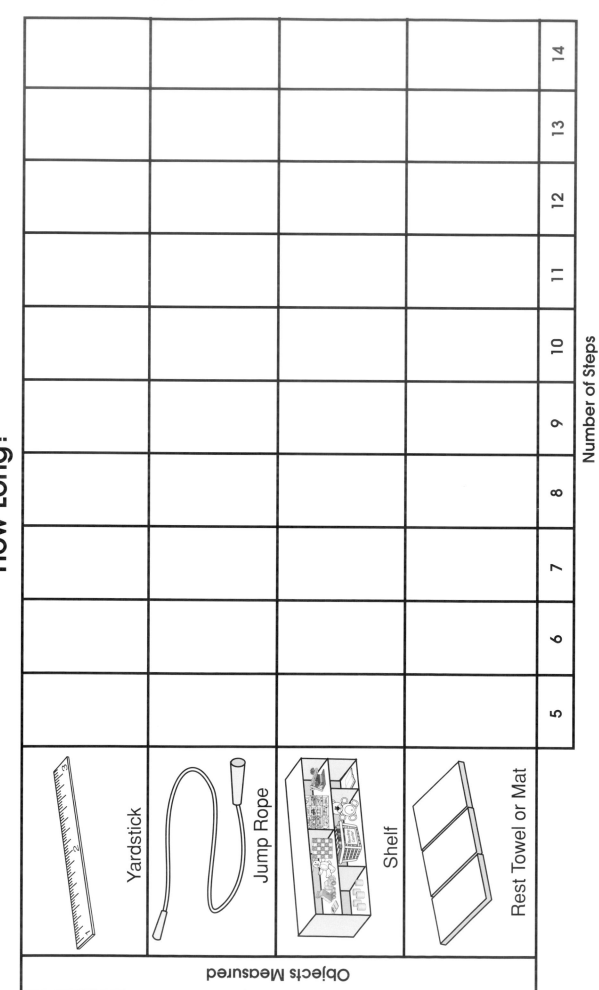

Objects Measured	5	6	7	8	9	10	11	12	13	14
Yardstick										
Jump Rope										
Shelf										
Rest Towel or Mat										

Number of Steps

©The Education Center, Inc. • *Gotta Have Graphs!* • TEC914

Note to the teacher: Use with "Walk It Off" on page 36.

On the Lookout for Shoes!

Dear Parent,

   Please help your child count how many pairs of shoes he/she finds around the house. There is space to tally below. Record the final number on the indicated line. Please return this completed tally to school tomorrow. Thanks for helping out!

I found _____ pairs of shoes.

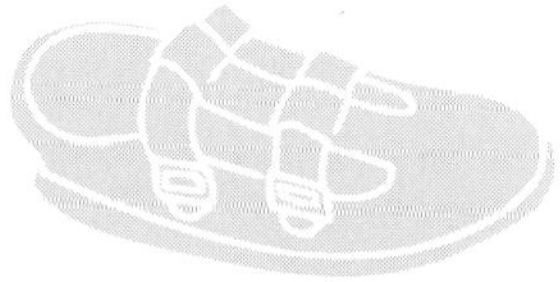

On the Lookout for Shoes!

Dear Parent,

   Please help your child count how many pairs of shoes he/she finds around the house. There is space to tally below. Record the final number on the indicated line. Please return this completed tally to school tomorrow. Thanks for helping out!

I found _____ pairs of shoes.

Please Pass the Graphs!

Take a bite out of graphing with these savory ideas.

Object Graph

Fabulous Fruit

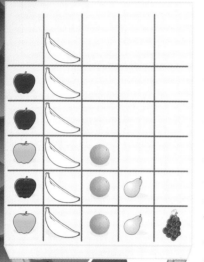

Sweet, juicy, healthy fruit makes for great snacking—and great graphing too! To prepare, send home with each child a copy of the parent note on page 43. On the designated day, prepare a graph by covering a tabletop with bulletin board paper. Gather your students and invite each child to show her piece of fruit. Next, have her place it on the paper according to type. Draw lines to make rows and columns to divide the fruits. When all the fruit is graphed, count, compare, and discuss the results with students. Lead them to draw conclusions such as the most popular fruit, the most unusual fruit, the largest and smallest fruit, and so forth. Vary the activity by having students graph the fruit by color. Later, invite each child to thoroughly wash her fruit and then enjoy it for a snack. So how many children like to eat apples or bananas?

Picture Graph

We Scream!

Lots of folks scream for ice cream, but do your students scream for chocolate or vanilla? Find out with a picture graph that smells *almost* good enough to eat! In advance, purchase powdered vanilla pudding mix and powdered chocolate milk mix. Use bulletin board paper to make a long, two-row graph labeled as shown; then display it within easy reach of your students. Duplicate the ice-cream scoop patterns on page 43 onto white construction paper to make a class supply. Cover a table with newspaper (for easy cleanup); then set out white and brown fingerpaint. Working with one small group at a time, have each child fingerpaint a scoop to resemble her preferred ice-cream flavor. While the paint is wet, have her sprinkle a small amount of the corresponding powdered mix onto her scoop. When the scoop is dry, have her cut it out and tape it to the graph in the corresponding row. Discuss the results as a class and enjoy the delicious aromas.

Picture Graph

Top This!

Mama mia—check out this graph! Explore students' pizza topping preferences with this pizza picture graph. To prepare, use bulletin board paper to create a six-column graph as shown. Then cut out a class supply of four-inch construction paper circles. Store the circles in a center with markers, crayons, glue, and a variety of craft materials to represent pizza toppings as shown. Invite each child to take a turn in the center decorating a pizza (circle) to represent his favorite pizza toppings. During a group time, have each child bring his completed pizza to the display; then sort them according to the number of toppings. Tape each group of slices to the blank graph to create a picture graph. Compare and discuss the results together. Mmm—what a pleasing pizza picture graph!

Toppings
green or black dots—olives
red circles—pepperoni
yellow tissue squares—cheese
brown semicircles—mushrooms
brown tissue bits—hamburger
green yarn—peppers
white yarn—onions

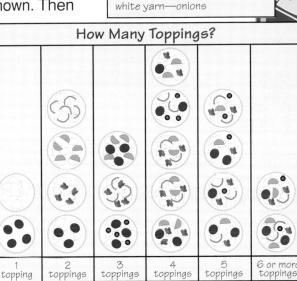

How Many Toppings?

| 1 topping | 2 toppings | 3 toppings | 4 toppings | 5 toppings | 6 or more toppings |

Picture Graph

What's for Dinner?

Serve up a hearty helping of graph skills and learn what your youngsters like to eat with this activity! To prepare, cut magazine photos of three kid-pleasing main dishes, such as spaghetti, fried chicken, and fish sticks. Duplicate the photos to make a class supply of each. Also use bulletin board paper to prepare a three-column graph as shown. During a circle time, discuss dinner choices and show students the prepared graph. Encourage each child to choose the food she prefers and then tape the appropriate picture in the corresponding column of the graph. Invite students to count and discuss the results as a group. For more challenge, ask students if they may have gotten different results if a food such as hamburgers were substituted for one of the choices.

| spaghetti | fried chicken | fish sticks |

Shapes Taste Great!

Crackers come in all shapes and sizes, so why not use a few for graphing? Obtain a supply of crackers in several shapes to match your attribute blocks. Display the boxes of crackers in a center with a bowl of matching attribute blocks in front of each. Also draw and label a corresponding tabletop graph on bulletin board paper. Invite a child at this center to look at each box of crackers and predict which she will like best. Have her put the matching attribute block on the graph. When each child has predicted, gather your group around the graph and discuss the results. While your children are out of the room, trace around each block on the graph; then put the blocks back in the bowl. Set aside the completed graph and prepare a second blank tabletop graph.

To complete the second graphing activity, open the boxes and pour the crackers into individual bowls. Place each bowl beside the corresponding bowl of attribute blocks. Invite each child to taste one of each cracker. Then have her put a matching attribute block on the graph to represent her favorite cracker. Gather students around this graph and discuss the results. Next, trace around each block and display both graphs. Compare the results; did anything change?

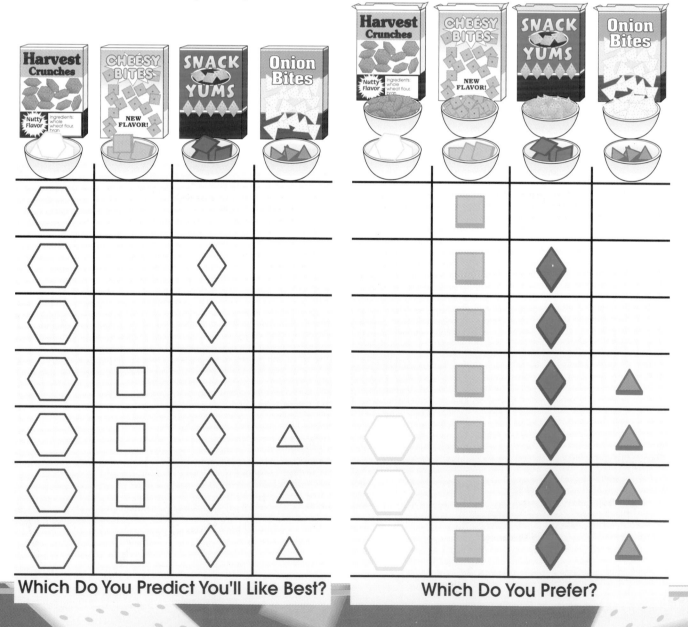

Which Do You Predict You'll Like Best?   **Which Do You Prefer?**

Dear Parent,
    We are learning about graphs in school. During our studies we will be graphing fruits we like to eat. Please help us on _____ by inviting your child to choose a small fruit he or she likes to eat. Help your child pack it to take to school. After our graphing activities, your child will eat the fruit for a snack.

Thanks for supporting your child's learning!

Ice-Cream Scoop Patterns
Use with "We Scream!" on page 40.

Keep It Movin'!

Travel near or far—you won't find better transportation graphing.

Venn Diagram

Planes and Trains

Have your students traveled on tracks? Have they soared through the skies? Find out with a Venn diagram! On a length of bulletin board paper, use two different colors of marker to draw two large intersecting circles; then label the diagram as shown. Next, give each student a small rectangle of colorful construction paper. Have him write his name on it and then tape a yarn loop handle to one side to resemble a suitcase. Display the prepared Venn diagram on a wall or bulletin board and gather students around it.

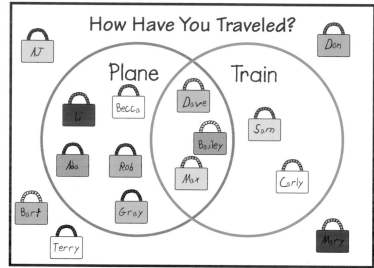

Ask one child at a time to tell whether he has traveled on a train, on a plane, on both, or on neither. Help him tape his suitcase inside the area that fits his answer. For example, if he has traveled on a plane but not on a train, he would put his suitcase inside the circle labeled "Plane." If he has traveled on both, he would put his suitcase in the intersection of the two circles. When everyone has contributed to the diagram, count and compare the number of names in each area. Give students an opportunity to share their experiences riding in a plane or train.

Object Graph

Vehicle Sorting Center

Rev up your center time with this vehicle sorting center! Gather a collection of toy vehicles. Then create a simple tabletop graph using masking tape to create the grid. Label the graph as

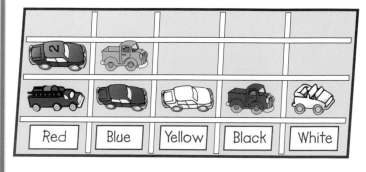

shown. Ask a pair of youngsters at this center to take a look at the collection and estimate which color category will have the most vehicles. Then have them sort the vehicles onto the tabletop graph by color. Was their estimate correct?

As a variation, have students sort the vehicles by type—such as plane, car, boat, truck, and train—instead of color.

By Land, Air, and Sea

How do vehicles go? Bet your students know! Set up a center where your youngsters sort vehicle pictures by where they travel. To prepare, duplicate the vehicle patterns on page 47 onto white construction paper. Color them as desired and cut apart the vehicles. Make a simple graphing mat similar to the one shown; then laminate all the vehicles and the mat for durability. Place the pieces at a center. Ask a child in this center to sort the vehicle patterns onto the mat, making a row for air travel, a row for land travel, and a row for water travel. Which category has the most vehicles? The fewest?

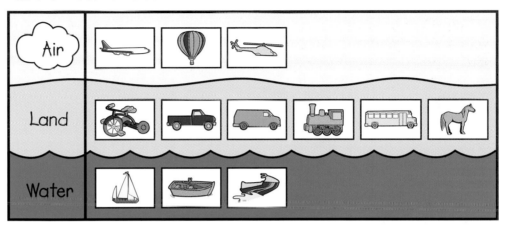

Picture Graph

"Wheel-y"?

Use the vehicle patterns on page 47 to make another great graph for center time. Duplicate the patterns, color them as desired, cut them out, and then laminate them for durability. Label a table-top with the two categories shown. Then ask a child at this center to sort the vehicle pictures into two rows—vehicles with wheels in one row and vehicles without wheels in the other row. Now your students are really on a roll!

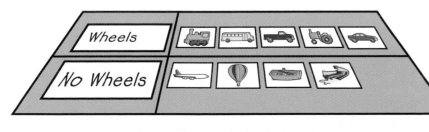

Symbolic Graph

What Is Your Favorite Transportation Tune?		
	Erin	
	Christopher	
Tanner	Emily	
Trent	Michael	Penny
Elizabeth	David	Yenna
Casey	HaoAnn	Andy
"Row, Row, Row Your Boat"	"The Wheels on the Bus"	"Down by the Station"

Transportation Tunes

Invite your young music lovers to vote on their favorite transportation tune! To begin, have a sing-along with such favorites as "Row, Row, Row Your Boat," "Down by the Station," and "The Wheels on the Bus." Then create a graph on a sheet of chart paper similar to the one shown. Label the bottom of each column with a different transportation song title. Ask each child to step up and write her name above her favorite tune. Count the votes for each song and then compare the graph results.

Bar Graph

Move It!

Transportation is all about moving people and things. Have your students explore various methods for moving classroom books as they make this bar graph. To begin, place a boxful of books across the room from your reading area or bookshelf. Ask students to brainstorm three different ways they could move the books to their proper location, such as in a toy dump truck, in a mini wagon, or by carrying the books. Label a length of bulletin board paper with the names or illustrations of the three methods. Then draw a numbered grid of lines above the words or drawings. Ask pairs or small groups to test each mode of transportation; then have a student color in the spaces on the graph to show you how many trips it took to move the books. Discuss which method was the most efficient and why.

How Many Trips?

Number of Trips — Type of Transportation

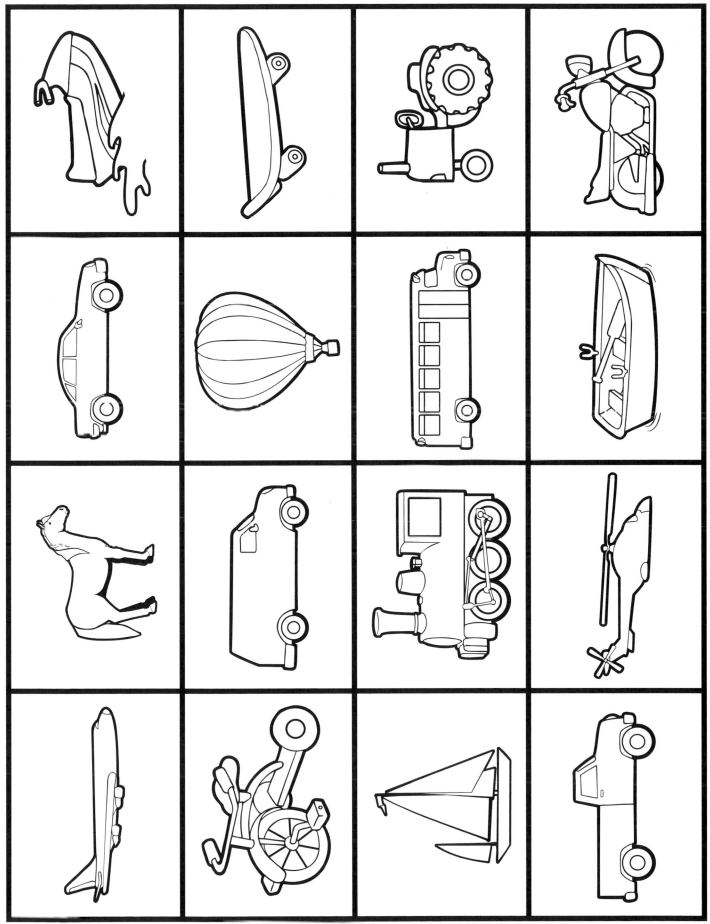

Fabulous Fairy Tales!

No need for a fairy godmother—youngsters will enjoy these graphing activities all on their own!

Picture Graph

If I Were in a Fairy Tale...

Do your youngsters see themselves as pretty princesses? Sly foxes? Sweet cookies? You'll find out when you create this class graph about fairy-tale characters! Ask each child to think of his answer to the question "If I were a fairy-tale character, who would I be?" Then have him draw a picture of himself as that character. On your chalkboard, create a number of columns.

As each child shares his picture, write the character's name at the bottom of one column. Have him attach his drawing to the board above the character name. Keep going until everyone has shared his picture and added it to your graph. (Add columns as necessary.) Discuss the results. Which character was most popular? Why?

If I Were A Fairy-Tale Character, I Would Be...

| Cinderella | The Gingerbread Man | The Wolf | Prince Charming | Little Red Hen | Sleeping Beauty | Hansel |

Picture Graph

Who's Scary?

Most—but not all—fairy tales have a scary character. Which type of scary character is most common? Find out with a graph that's not so scary to create! Make one copy of the character patterns on page 50. Duplicate the book pattern on page 50 to make a class supply. Glue the character patterns down one side of a length of bulletin board paper as shown; then draw lines to create rows. Give each child a book pattern. Ask one child at a time to name a fairy tale. Have her write the title on her book pattern. Then have her tape the pattern to the graph in the row that shows the type of scary character found in that tale. After everyone has added to the graph, look at the results. Do more tales have witches, wolves, or someone wicked?

Who's Scary?

witch

wolf

giant

wicked person

no scary character

Symbolic Graph

Character Categories

Keep this graph going throughout your fairy-tale unit; then examine it at the end of your study to find out just who these fairy-tale characters are! On a sheet of chart paper, create three columns and label them as shown. After reading each fairy tale, have student volunteers write the characters' names on sticky notes and post them in the corresponding columns. Periodically have students predict whether there will eventually be more animal characters or human characters.

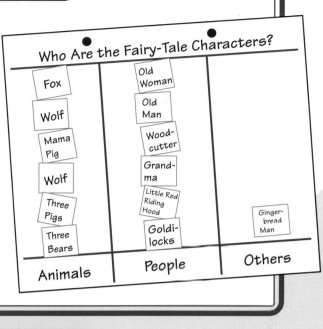

Who Are the Fairy-Tale Characters?

Animals	People	Others
Fox	Old Woman	
Wolf	Old Man	
Mama Pig	Wood-cutter	
Wolf	Grand-ma	
Three Pigs	Little Red Riding Hood	Ginger-bread Man
Three Bears	Goldi-locks	

Glyph

Favorite Tales

Here's a unique way for youngsters to share which fairy tales are their favorites. Give each child a copy of the castle pattern on page 51. Ask her to keep her favorite fairy tale in mind as she listens to the instructions below and adds details to her castle. When the glyphs are finished, invite youngsters to share them in small groups. Or, as a challenge, have each child show her completed castle to a partner *without* telling her partner what her favorite fairy tale is. Have the partner analyze the glyph to guess the tale. As an extension, help students use the glyphs to graph data such as how many tales had wolves and children.

Glyph Guide

Does your fairy tale have a wolf? If yes, draw a single door. If no, draw a double door.

Does your fairy tale have a set of three (such as three pigs or three bears)? If yes, draw three windows across the center. If no, draw one big window.

Does your fairy tale have a witch? If yes, draw a flag on top of one of the turrets.

Does your fairy tale have children? If yes, draw flowers on the ground outside the castle.

Character and Book Patterns
Use with "Who's Scary?" on page 48.

witch

wolf

wicked person

giant

no scary character

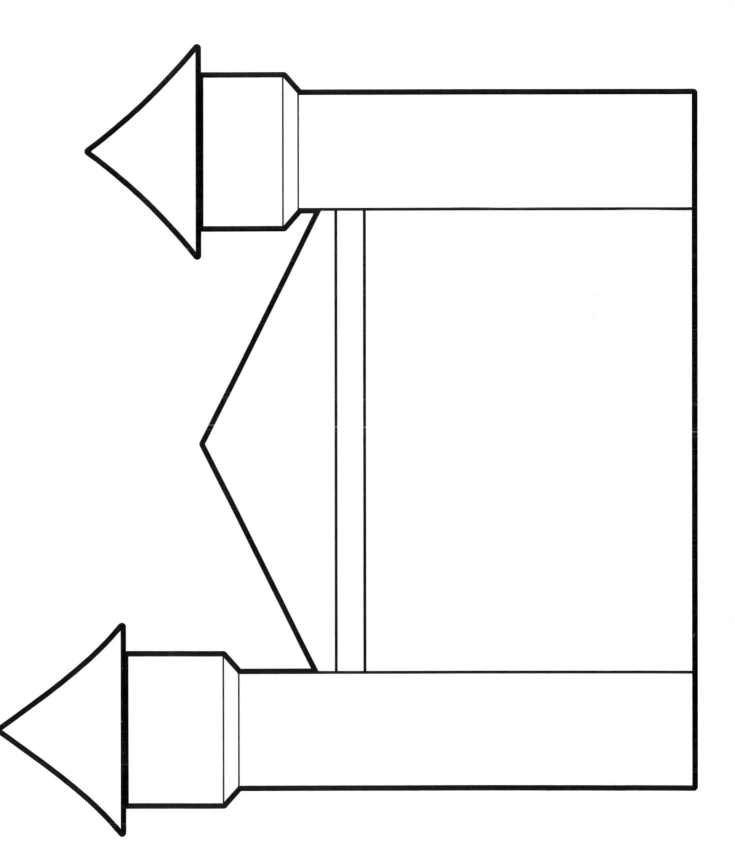

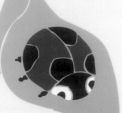

Going Buggy

Flit and flutter right through graphing ideas that will have your youngsters beggin' for bugs!

Picture Graph

Ladybug, Ladybug

You'll be seeing spots after youngsters create these pretty bugs! Copy the ladybug pattern (page 54) onto white construction paper for each child. Have the child color his bug his choice of red, orange, or yellow. Then provide cotton swabs and black paint for the child to use in making spots on his bug. (Limit the number of spots to a maximum of 12.) After the paint dries, have the children cut out their bugs, sort them, and then use them to make a simple class graph as shown. Invite your students to decide whether to graph the ladybugs by color or by the number of spots. Or for more challenge, do both!

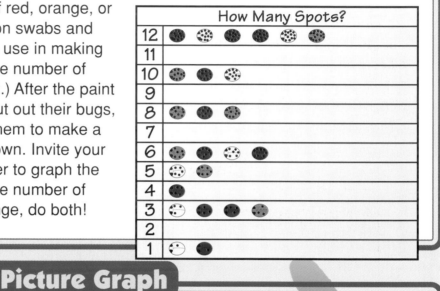

How Many Spots?

Picture Graph

A Tasty Graph?

Bees are a special insect because they provide a tasty treat for us to eat! Try this delicious graphing activity to help your youngsters discover the different flavors of honey as well as practice their bar graph skills. Ahead of time, collect several honey flavors such as the ones shown. Set up a station for each type with a small dish of honey and a class supply of one-inch bread cubes. Have each student visit each station and use a separate bread cube to taste each type of honey. When a child has sampled each type of honey, give her a copy of the honeypot pattern on page 54. Instruct the child to color and cut out the pattern; then help her write the name of her favorite flavor on the honeypot. Make a class graph using the honeypots to show the relative popularity of the various honey flavors. Graphing never tasted so sweet!

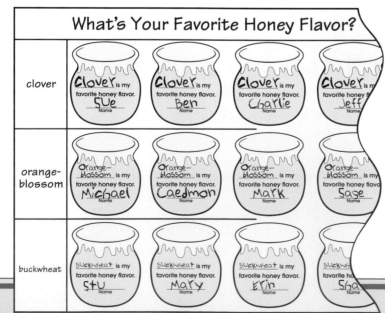

52

Insects! Insects! Everywhere!

Help students see just how many insects are around us with the following fun data collection activity. To prepare, construct on a large sheet of bulletin board paper the graph shown. Next, make five copies of page 55. Cut out each insect pattern. Also gather a class supply of sentence strips.

To complete the activity, give one insect pattern, one sentence strip, a sheet of paper, and a pencil to each student. Have the student color and then glue his insect to the center of his strip. With the insect pattern in the front, place the sentence strip around the student's head to make a headband. Cut off any excess sentence strip and staple to secure. Place the headband back on the student. Next, have students sort themselves by type of insect. Then take your students on a nature walk to see how many of the assigned insects they can find. Remind students of safety rules and instruct them not to touch any insect. Direct each student to make a tally mark on his sheet when he sees the appropriate insect. Return to the classroom and have students regroup by insect. Have one member from the grasshopper group come to the graph and color one block to the right of the grasshopper for each grasshopper counted. Repeat the process for each remaining insect group. Conclude by having students discuss why some insects were discovered in higher numbers than others.

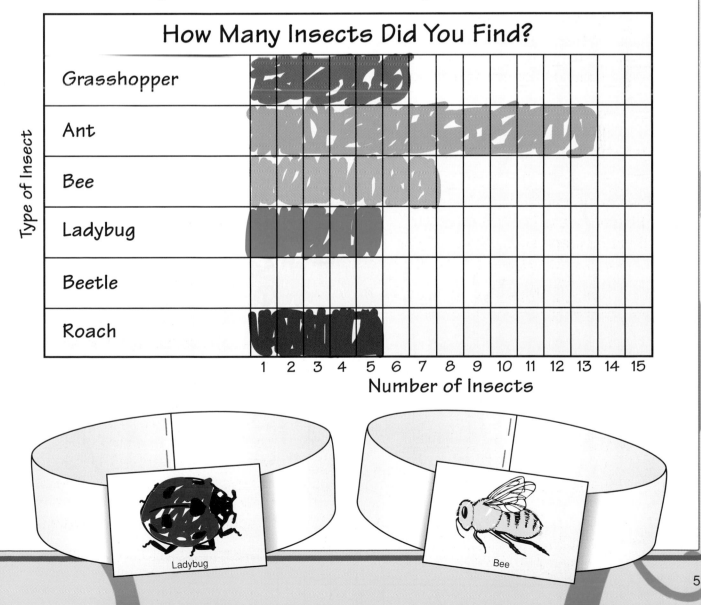

How Many Insects Did You Find?

Type of Insect: Grasshopper, Ant, Bee, Ladybug, Beetle, Roach

Number of Insects: 1 2 3 4 5 6 7 8 9 10 11 12 13 14 15

Ladybug

Bee

Ladybug Pattern

Use with "Ladybug, Ladybug" on page 52.

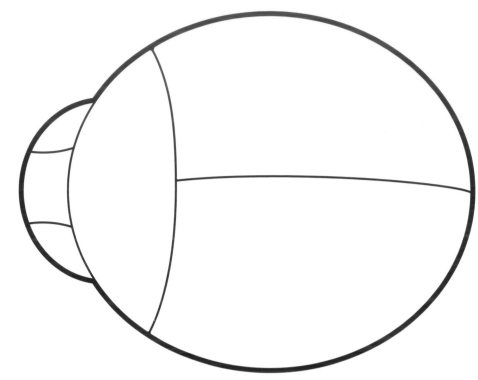

Honeypot Pattern

Use with "A Tasty Graph?" on page 52.

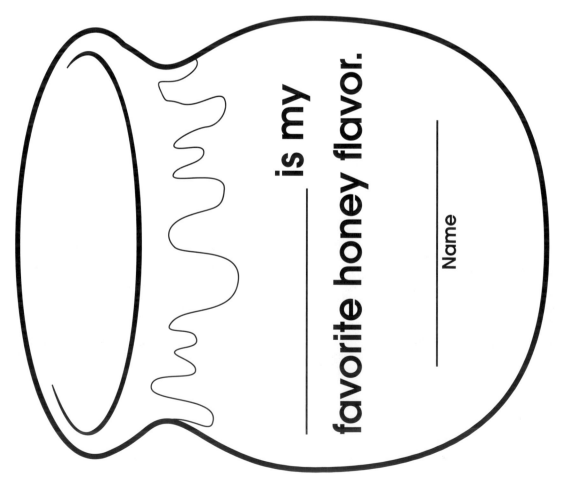

_____ is my favorite honey flavor.

Name

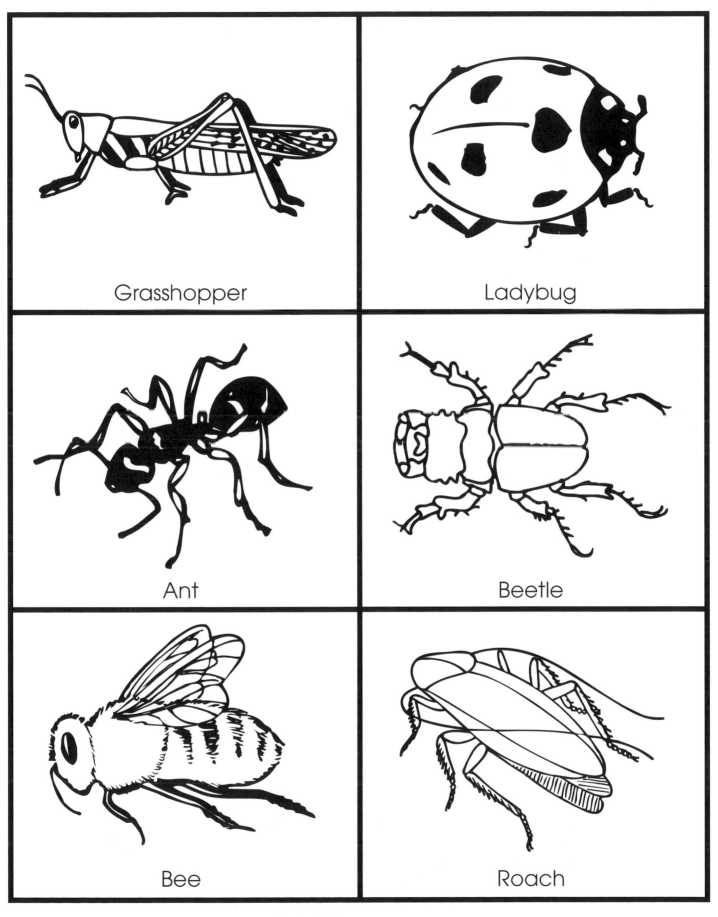

Grasshopper

Ladybug

Ant

Beetle

Bee

Roach

Oceans of Graphs

Ahoy! Get your youngsters graphing with this seaworthy series of ideas!

Picture Graph

At the Beach

Everyone has a favorite beach activity, whether it's flying a kite, building a sand castle, or hunting for shells. To prepare this wall graph, write the graphing question on a sentence strip and attach the strip, as shown, to a wall. Cut a few shorter lengths of sentence strip to use for the row labels. Then ask each of your youngsters to draw a picture of herself enjoying her favorite beach pastime. Have each child share her picture with the group before you label the rows and tape the pictures to the wall graph. Discuss the results with the class. Which activity is the most popular?

Object Graph

A Fishy Center

This center activity helps little ones with sorting and graphing skills, and it's delicious too! To prepare, ask parents to donate Goldfish crackers in three different flavors, such as cheddar, pizza, and pretzel. Mix the crackers together in a large bowl. Place the bowl at a center, along with a supply of three-ounce paper cups. Make one copy of the graphing sheet on page 58; then label the copy with the three types of crackers you have. Duplicate the programmed sheet and add the copies to the center.

Invite a child at this center to scoop up a cupful of Goldfish crackers. Then have him sort the crackers by type onto a copy of the graphing sheet and examine the results. After you've checked his work, encourage him to eat his crackers. Mmm! Math is yummy!

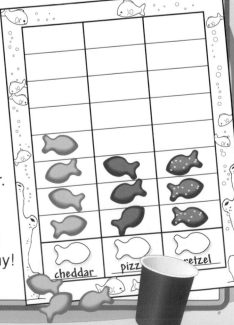

Object Graph

Shells in the Sand

Bring the beach to your classroom—or at least the sand and shells! Partially fill a sensory table or large plastic tub with play sand. In the sand, bury a collection of real seashells, making sure there are three or four distinct types of shells. Then use lengths of yarn to create a grid on a nearby tabletop. Ask a small group of youngsters at this center to use sand shovels or their hands to dig for shells. Have them sort the shells by type and lay them on the grid in rows to create an object graph. When the group has finished, ask them to look at the graph and discuss the results. Guide them to use the words *most, fewest,* and *equal.*

Bar Graph

Favorite Sea Animals

Which sea animal is your class's favorite? Find out with a fun activity that will lead to a colorful bar graph! To prepare, create an eight-column graph on a large sheet of white bulletin board paper as shown. Next, make a copy of the sea animal patterns on page 59. Cut out each pattern; then post each pattern in a separate column at the bottom of the graph. Next, make an enlarged copy of each pattern on page 59. Post each enlarged sea animal pattern in a different location in the room.

Gather your students; then point out each enlarged sea animal posted around the room. Direct each student to stand beneath the sea animal that's his favorite. Next, assign a color to each animal group. Have each child in the first group come up to your prepared graph and color the section above the appropriate sea animal on the graph with a crayon matching her group's color. Invite others in that group to each color a successive section; then continue with other groups until every child has colored a section. The resulting bar graph will show the class's favorite!

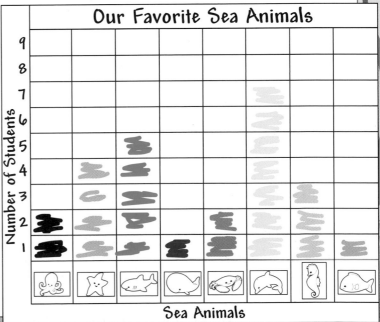

57

Note to the teacher: Use with "A Fishy Center" on page 56.

Animals Abound!

Moo, neigh, meow, squeak—these animal graphs are quite unique!

Picture Graph

Name __June__   Picture graph

How Does It Move?

	panda	
	horse	
cow	goose	snake
lion	ostrich	snail
bee	dog	penguin	porpoise
ant	zebra	chicken	seal
six legs	four legs	two legs	no legs

How Does It Move?

On four legs, two legs, or no legs at all—animals move in lots of ways! Use this picture graph to illustrate some of the ways animals move. Duplicate the graph (page 62) and the animal cards (page 63) for each child; then store the copies in a center. Invite each child visiting this center to color and cut apart her animal cards. Encourage each student to examine her cards and sort them by the number of legs each animal has. Next, have her place each set onto the graph in the appropriate column, check her own work, and then glue them in place. For more challenge, engage students in a discussion of other animal features or attributes. If desired, duplicate additional sets of cards and blank graphs so students may graph the animals according to other attributes.

Venn Diagram

Where Does It Live?

Now that your students know how many legs animals have, have them decide where animals live with this Venn diagram. In advance, draw and label two intersecting circles on a sheet of chart paper as shown. Enlarge by 25 percent a copy of the animal cards on page 63; then color and cut them out. Post the diagram in your circle area and gather students around it. With your class, discuss the various places animals live, making sure to include farms and zoos. Show the group an animal card and encourage them to decide where the animal lives. (Be prepared for some lively discussion!) Invite a volunteer to tape the card in the appropriate area of the diagram. Repeat with the remaining cards. When the diagram is complete, count how many animals are in each category, including "both" and "neither." Encourage students to talk about the results, and add more animals if desired.

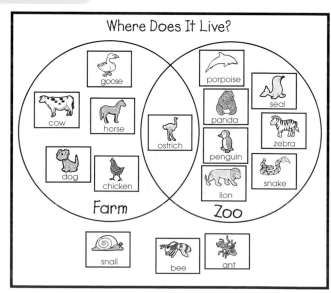

Glyph

My Favorite Pet

So what kinds of animals do your students keep as pets? Or what kinds of animals would they choose as pets? Find out with this great glyph! In advance, write the glyph guide below on a sheet of chart paper. Give each child a sheet of drawing paper and crayons, and explain that you are going to give students a series of directions to draw an animal head that contains information about their pets. Then slowly read aloud the glyph guide to direct their drawing. When the glyphs are complete, discuss the information revealed. Then help students create a class graph of the data revealed in the glyphs, such as type of pet or inside/outside pets.

Glyph Guide

If you have a pet, draw a round head. ○ If you want or can imagine having a pet, draw a square head. ☐

If your pet lives inside, draw an oval nose. ⬭ If your pet lives outside, draw a triangle nose. △

If your pet is a dog, draw and color spotted ears.

If your pet is a cat, draw and color striped ears.

If your pet is another kind of animal, draw and color solid-colored ears.

If your pet is heavy, draw open eyes.

If your pet is light, draw closed eyes.

If your pet has a tail, draw a red mouth.

If your pet does not have a tail, draw a pink mouth.

If your pet has fur, draw squiggly whiskers.

If your pet has another body covering (scales, feathers, or fins), draw straight whiskers.

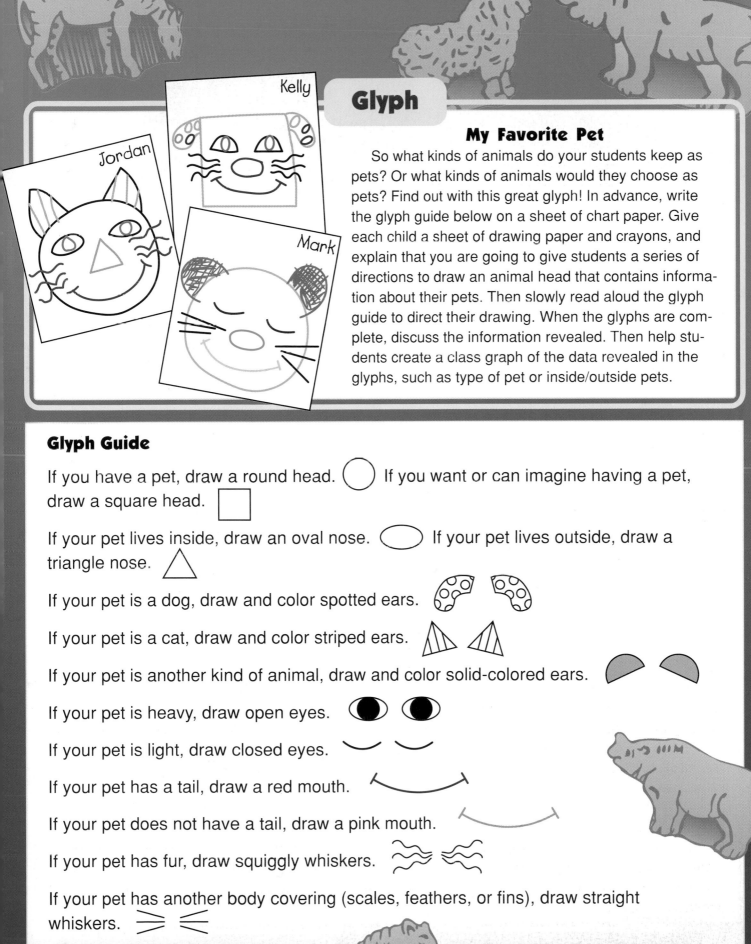

How Does It Move?

six legs	four legs	two legs	no legs

Note to the teacher: Use with "How Does It Move?" on page 60.

Use with "How Does It Move?" and "Where Does It Live?" on page 60.

goose • porpoise • seal • ant

bee • panda • dog • zebra

snail • penguin • horse • lion

chicken • cow • ostrich • snake

Gotta Have Graphs!

Over 60 Kid-Pleasing, Curriculum-Based Graphing Activities and Data Displays

More great math books from *The Mailbox*®

Managing Editors: Jan Trautman, Allison E. Ward
Editor at Large: Diane Badden
Writers: Deborah Carter, Ada Goren, Lucia Kemp Henry, Angie Kutzer, Suzanne Moore
Copy Editors: Sylvan Allen, Karen Brewer Grossman, Amy Kirtley-Hill, Karen L. Huffman, Debbie Shoffner
Cover Artist: Clevell Harris
Art Coordinator: Pam Crane
Artists: Pam Crane, Nick Greenwood, Ivy L. Koonce, Sheila Krill, Clint Moore, Greg D. Rieves, Rebecca Saunders, Barry Slate, Stuart Smith, Donna K. Teal
Typesetters: Lynette Dickerson, Mark Rainey

President, The Mailbox Book Company™: Joseph C. Bucci
Director of Book Planning and Development: Chris Poindexter
Book Development Managers: Elizabeth H. Lindsay, Thad McLaurin, Susan Walker
Curriculum Director: Karen P. Shelton
Traffic Manager: Lisa K. Pitts
Librarian: Dorothy C. McKinney
Editorial and Freelance Management: Karen A. Brudnak
Editorial Training: Irving P. Crump
Editorial Assistants: Terrie Head, Hope Rodgers, Jan E. Witcher

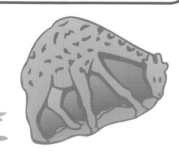